Whales
and
Dolphins

WHALES AND DOLPHINS

Part one
Whales and dolphins in the Animal World

Part two
Whales and dolphins in Our World

Creative workshop

Whales and Dolphins in the Animal World

A dolphin's snout is called a beak. The distinctive curvature of its mouth gives this small cetacean a jovial expression.

Dolphins, exuberant wake-riders

Playful, talkative and affectionate mammals, dolphins inhabit virtually all the world's oceans. In large or small schools, their high level of intelligence can be seen both in the strict upbringing they give their calves and the way they hunt for food.

Atlantic spotted dolphins (*Stenella frontalis*) prefer the warm, clear waters of the Bahamas.

olphins, which number some 30 species, belong to the largest family of cetaceans, the Delphinidae. These marine animals inhabit all the world's seas, with the exception of colder waters. Oceanic dolphins travel in large schools while smaller schools of dolphins are found near the shore; but whatever the size of the school, its make-up rarely differs: in the middle females suckling their calves

Even oceanic dolphins venture near the shore.

Relaxing in the doldrums of the Atlantic, bottlenosed dolphins take a well-earned rest. They are never sheltered from violent storms in the open sea.

In the warm Mexican waters of Lower California, dolphins savour the pleasures of communal life.

are protected by the juveniles and adult males who keep watch. These groups of playful mammals can cover several hundred nautical miles in a year.

Free love

In summer, during the breeding season, neighbouring schools establish closer contact and the males take a more active interest in the females. For several weeks, they perform

Even at night, dolphins play or remain alert, watching their surroundings.

outstanding acrobatic feats to impress the mature females, who are soon won over. Dolphins lose no time in pairing up to mate, caressing, rubbing sides and chasing each other before an extremely brief copulation. However, they do not remain with one mate and have numerous sexual partners before the end of the breeding season.

A strict yet practical upbringing

Young calves receive a fairly strict upbringing, designed to lay the foundations for communal life. For its first five years, the calf remains in close contact with its mother, who indicates any change of direction with her body. If the calf disobeys and strays from her side, she catches up with it and dispenses a severe physical punishment, making it cry out in pain. This is necessary to imbue the young rebel with a keen sense of discipline and a fear of sharks, which have a taste for young dolphins. Groups of juvenile dolphins move out to the fringes of the

Dolphins, surfacing for air, perform some graceful leaps.

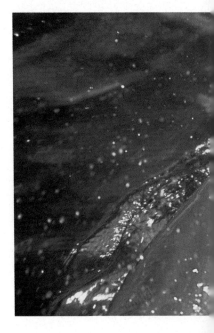

Before mating, dolphins indulge in lengthy caresses, particularly rubbing sides.

▼ Even dolphins do not find it easy to sleep in the water and must continually take care not to go under and drown. The obvious solution is to allow only one half of the brain to rest, while the other maintains the ideal position for the body so that it stays on the surface and keeps the blowhole (the dolphin's nostril) closed in case of waves. Dolphins alternately rest the left and right sides of their brain for around two hours at a time to obtain a total of eight hours''sleep'.

Young dolphins enjoy emulating their parents by competing in races.

Even a branch can provide dolphins with the chance for a little fun.

school to practise hunting techniques, accompanied by an adult who will call them to order if they misbehave and round them up if danger threatens.

Learning through play

Keen to emulate their elders, young dolphins take part in friendly contests during which they chase one another, jostle, butt heads and nibble one another. These games are highly instructive:

Bottlenosed dolphins are agile acrobats and, of all the dolphins, seem to enjoy playing the most.

These dolphins spend a large part of their day cavorting in the sunlit waters of the Caribbean sea.

When approaching the shore, groups of dolphins send their scouts ahead.

like primates, they are rehearsing behavioural patterns – attacks and mating displays – that will be very useful in adult life.

Vital communication

Learning about life in this way would not be possible without the dolphins' highly-developed mode of communication, which is extremely unusual in the animal kingdom. Dolphins communicate using a

Young dolphins – in a close-knit group – venture far from their school to explore their surroundings. An adult keeps a close watch on them.

complex language of whistles that vary in intensity and frequency. The males whistle or sing to attract females during the breeding season and to warn the group of danger. The mothers whistle for days on end after the birth of their calves to accustom them to the sound of their 'voice'. Each dolphin is also identified by its own distinctive inflection  which enables it to communicate with other individuals.

Dolphins whistle frequently, even on the surface of the water.

Dolphins remain in close vocal contact with other members of their group.

A living sonar system

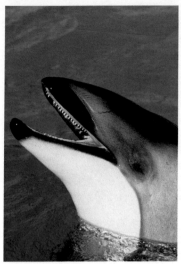

The Atlantic white-sided dolphin raises its head above water.

In addition to their continual whistling, dolphins also constantly emit 'clicking' sounds. These clicks are produced by the pharynx and amplified by an oily organ, called the melon. When bounced off obstacles, these clicks form sound waves which return as echoes and are picked up by the dolphin. Its brain analyses the time taken for the sound waves to return and develops an

In the shallow waters of the Great Barrier Reef, the dolphin's sonar system is an invaluable tool, enabling it to avoid dangerous reefs.

This group of beaters has located a large shoal of fish with their high-performance sonar system. After a short consultation, the hunt is on.

Black or dark grey pilot whales, with their large rounded head and well-developed flippers, are very distinctive in appearance. Because of their size — some attain a length of 6 metres — they are often placed in the suborder of 'toothed whales', but they actually belong to the large Delphinidae family. Fond of frolicking in temperate and subpolar waters, these giant dolphins feed at night, hunting squid that have ventured to the surface.

At 40 kilometres per hour, dolphins can rival the speed of any fish they hunt.

extremely accurate picture of its surroundings: this enables these small cetaceans to 'see' in murky water and even at the dead of night.

Two square meals a day for these outstanding hunters

Early in the morning and late in the afternoon, dolphins organize hunting parties. Once they have located the shoals of fish by sonar, a vocal signal is given and 'beaters' launch into action. The fish, trapped within a noisy, vicious circle, have no option but to close ranks and rise to the surface. The entire group of dolphins can then eat their fill. Each creature can devour approximately 20 kilograms of fish per day, a staple diet that may be supplemented by squid or shrimp. Other marine predators, such as the tuna or the frigate bird, take advantage of this strategy used by groups of dolphins to enjoy a free meal.

In the silence of the oceans, killer whales pose a lethal threat to their prey as they are experts at keeping a low profile.

Killer whales, ocean predators

The killer whale is in a class of its own in the extended family of the cetaceans. A relentless hunter and one of the ocean's greatest predators, the killer whale is the only marine mammal that attacks its own relatives – dolphins and baleen whales – with impunity.

Fish and marine mammals prefer to give killer whales and their fearsome jaws an extremely wide berth.

Also called the grampus or orc, the killer whale is the largest member of the Delphinidae family. This black and white cetacean lives in small isolated family pods, or groups which only meet in the breeding season.

Residents and transients

There are two distinct types of killer whale which differ in their behaviour, diet and physical appearance: residents and transients. Although transients are recognizable by their more pointed dorsal fin and prefer to roam vast distances in smallish pods (four or five), residents stay closer to the shore in pods of 20 to 30. Residents are the, more sociable animals, and they tend to sing and play more often than their oceanic counterparts. They also never stay underwater for longer than five minutes, although transients will happily dive down for up to 15 minutes at a time.

A killer whale can reach record speeds of 50 kilometres per hour.

The males, recognizable by their large dorsal fin, prefer to keep their distance from their pod.

Killer whales are hardy creatures ideally suited to all the world's oceans and seas. They have even been spotted on occasion in fresh water: in 1931, for example, a female, 4 metres in length, swam up the Columbia river, in Oregon, for over 180 kilometres and stayed there for almost a year before returning to the sea. It is not surprising, therefore, that killer whales range from the Great Ice Barrier to the tropical seas. They show a marked preference, however, for colder waters.

The largest ocean predator

Transient and resident killer whales also differ in their diet: the former hunt fish almost exclusively, while the latter enjoy a much more varied diet, feeding on fish, sharks, squid, seabirds, turtles, penguins, dolphins and whales. Anything that swims in the ocean may end up in the belly of a transient killer whale which, when drawing near

The teeth of the killer whale bring to mind instruments of torture.

This killer whale is 'spyhopping': it raises its head from the water to survey its surroundings for potential prey.

Diving in the cold waters of British Columbia, transients avoid being given away by their blow (spout).

to the shore to feed on seals, walruses and sea lions, runs the very real risk of becoming stranded.

A softly-softly approach when hunting cetaceans

Like their close relatives, the dolphins, oceanic killer whales hunt fish and squid with the help of 'beaters' that remain in continual vocal contact. They apply a completely different strategy, however, when

The killer whale's dark colouring enables it to pass unnoticed in the greyish water.

In the Atlantic fogs, killer whales on the prowl near the shore can only be detected by their spout.

Killer whales hunt 'big game' in large pods.

attacking other cetaceans, as all cetaceans have extremely keen hearing. The patrol works in complete silence and spouts are kept to a strict minimum when reaching areas frequented by dolphins or baleen whales. Because of their huge bulk, large baleen whales are formidable adversaries that can only be defeated if the killer whales are inventive in their battle tactics.

The killer whale attacks single-mindedly, bearing down on its prey, confident of its unbeatable speed and powerful jaws.

Surrounded by a cloud of spray formed by its powerful blow, a killer whale patrols the chilly waters.

The hapless victims of the killer whale often see it too late, discovering the strength of its jaws to their cost. Around 50 conical teeth, curving inwards, enable killer whales to chew up a baleen whale with disconcerting ease or literally crush seals, sea lions or dolphins. This is because, when they close their mouths, the teeth in the upper jaw interlock exactly with the teeth in the lower jaw.

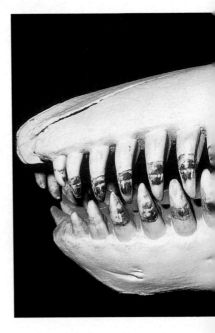

Killer whales versus baleen whales, a tactical battle

When attacking, killer whales display remark-able organizational skills. A group of attackers im-mobilizes their victim by shredding its flippers while others immediately attack its head. Their aim is to reach the whale's tongue – a particularly sensitive organ – by biting its lips, forcing it to open its mouth. In the violent struggle that ensues, it is not unusual for one or several of the killer whales to be injured or occasionally killed by a single blow from the victim's tail. However, baleen whales rarely win this fight to the death as killer whales will only attack after weighing up all the risks. Their only chance for escape is to take refuge in shallow water, where they appear to be less vulnerable. Seals and other sea lions are even less likely to survive when attacked by killer whales, which can reach speeds of up to 55 kilometres per hour. Unless diverted by the timely appearance of an appetizing shoal of fish, these black and white killers never show their victims any mercy.

The dorsal fin of male killer whales can attain a height of 2 metres.

29

Rising from unfathomable oceanic depths, the sperm whale breaks the surface with its massive head, exposing its blowhole, the opening or nostril through which it breathes.

Sperm whales, masters of the deep

In the gloom of the ocean, the massive sperm whale or cachalot engages in titanic fights with giant squids. It has to dive to a depth of more than 2000 metres, an unbeaten record for marine mammals, to locate these terrifying creatures.

Although the undisputed lord of the deep, the sperm whale does not object to taking a brief rest on the surface.

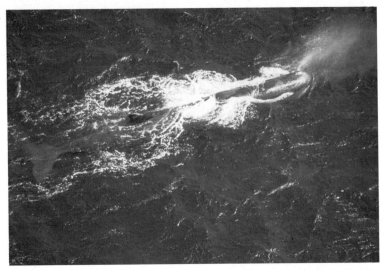

Sperm whales have an unmistakable blow or spout, that is always angled forward and can attain a length of 2 to 5 metres.

The massive sperm whale, which can attain a length of 20 metres and weight of 70 tonnes, is the largest member of the suborder of toothed whales. With its huge squarish head, which accounts for over a third of its total body length, this whale has one of the most remarkable and unmistakable profiles of any marine mammal. Seasoned travellers, sperm whales occur in all the oceans, although

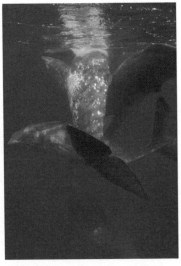

Sperm whales bear the scars of their deep-sea fights.

Young sperm whales learning to dive.

they prefer the oceanic depths to coastal areas and warm and temperate waters to the colder polar waters. Although they feed on jellyfish, tuna, cod and small sharks on the surface, the most common prey of sperm whales is the giant squid, which they hunt at the bottom of the sea.

Over a tonne of squid each day

Sperm whales eat over a tonne of squid each day,

No giant squid has ever been seen alive. Only the remains of corpses have been found washed up on beaches or in the stomach of sperm whales.

hunting their prey at depths of between 500 and 2000 metres. Lying in wait in the deep-sea darkness, the sperm whale uses its sonar system to locate squid and deep-sea fish. As soon as a potential victim appears within reach, probably attracted by the cetacean's whitish lips, the sperm whale attacks, swallowing its prey whole. But giant squids – which can attain a length of more than 10 metres – do not

When they are not diving, sperm whales swim in groups near the surface.

Powerful tale flukes help sperm whales dive to a depth of several thousand metres.

A sperm whale disappears in the sunset off the coast of the Azores to hunt for food. After a two-hour dive, it resurfaces at exactly the same spot.

In breeding schools, the females frequently surround their calves to educate them and protect them from danger.

▼ Several tonnes of a liquid fat called spermaceti are housed in the sperm whale's massive head and can be used as a type of ballast when diving deeper than 2000 metres. By slowing down the circulation of blood in its huge snout, the sperm whale can set or liquefy this fat. When congealed, the fat increases in density and the sperm whale heads straight for the bottom; when liquefied, it decreases in density, enabling the sperm whale to rise like a balloon.

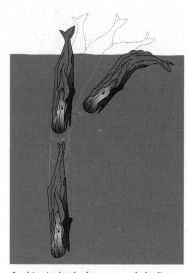

Arching its back, the sperm whale dives for the bottom.

always give up without a fight. They may react by clutching the sperm whale in their powerful tentacles.
A savage fight ensues and, although the sperm whales always win, they are often badly scarred by these deep-sea encounters.

All adult males have harems

Families of sperm whales live in groups or herds of 10 to 30 individuals, including calves of both sexes and females, which remain together for many years. Each herd is dependent on one adult male, which rejoins its family in spring, for the breeding season. The rest of the time, this lone bull leads a solitary existence. After some ten years spent with their mothers, the young males cut free and leave the herd in their turn. Until the age of 25, they travel in small bachelor herds, roaming the oceans in search of sexual encounters. After the age of 25, they turn their back on this life of adventure, and begin to form their own harem, which can comprise as many as 30 females.

Sperm whales usually live in the open sea. They also inhabit coastal areas bordering deep seas, as in the vicinity of New Zealand.

Virtually half out of the water, the grey whale (*Eschrichtius robustus*) surveys its surroundings, on the lookout for a travelling companion.

Baleen whales, long-distance travellers

Gentle giants of the sea, baleen whales spend their time feeding during the summer when the icy polar waters are teeming with thousands of tiny shrimps. In winter, they cross thousands of kilometres to breed in the temperate waters of warmer seas.

The blue whale (*Balaenoptera musculus*) is the largest animal the Earth has ever known.

Baleen whales are very large animals, the smallest of which easily exceeds 10 metres in length. The blue whale or Sibbald's rorqual is by far the biggest member of this family: with its long spindle-shaped body, it is the largest animal that has ever lived on Earth (making even the largest dinosaurs look small). The blue whale can attain a length of 30 metres and weight of 200 tonnes. In the case of this gentle giant, and unlike many other species of animal, the female is slightly larger than the male.

In the vast blue expanse of the ocean, a humpback whale surfaces for air.

A collection of sea creatures hitching a ride

Most baleen whales are infested with thousands of crustaceans, which are attached to their skin or to the horny fringed plates or baleen inside their mouth. The most common and highly visible of these guests are barnacles, small crustaceans enclosed by a hard shell. They do no harm to these large cetaceans and are ideally placed to feast on the leftovers from their giant hosts' meals. Barnacles

Rorquals have a characteristically small dorsal fin and a long slender body.

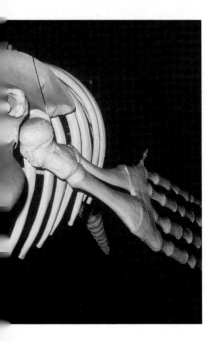

Baleen whales are descended from land mammals which resembled wolves. Some 50 million years ago, they gradually began to swim in the seas. Called ambulocetus, these intermediary whales had an elongated head and four powerful limbs, the forelimbs remaining well developed, as in this skeleton of a humpback whale. After a further ten million years, they divided into the two groups that are now known as mysticetes (baleen whales) and odontocetes (toothed whales).

(each measuring around a centimetre) also feed on plankton. In total, humpback whales (*Megaptera novaeangliae*), provide a home for around 500 kilograms of these sea creatures in addition to the many other crustaceans which also take advantage of this unique mode of transport. The patterns they form on the whale's body are never the same and can therefore be used to identify individual whales.

Barnacles prefer to attach themselves to baleen whales' callosities.

Each baleen whale can be distinguished from its counterparts by the particular pattern formed by the small crustaceans, called barnacles, clinging to its body.

The bowhead or Greenland right whale (*Balaena mysticetus*) has a thick layer of blubber which protects it from the cold waters of the Atlantic.

A thick layer of insulating fat

The enormous bulk of baleen whales keeps them safe from numerous predators and enables them to withstand the icy cold of the polar seas. Beneath their fairly thin skin, they have a layer of blubber, 50 centimetres thick, which may account for 40 percent of the animal's total body weight. This covering of fat provides total thermal protection, enabling whales to endure the cold and avoid overheating.

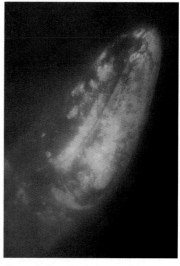

Grey whale in the dark seas of the frozen North.

The blue whale, or Sibbald's rorqual, has the most impressive tail. Its width is equal to a quarter of the animal's total length, in other words, between 5 and 7 metres.

Here, a grey whale rests its tail on the seabed and lifts its head above the surface.

This is because the blubber is criss-crossed by a network of large blood vessels. When the whale's temperature rises, as a result of activity or time spent in warm water, for example, these blood vessels dilate and the blood flow beneath the skin lowers the body temperature. When resting, or in extremely cold water, the whale restricts the blood flow through these veins and can fully benefit from the protection provided by its blubber.

In the cold, productive waters of Alaska, humpback whales (*Megaptera novaeangliae*) dive to feed.

Although extremely fond of shrimp, common rorquals will happily feed on small fish.

An appetite to match their bulk

To maintain their reserves of fat, baleen whales must eat between 1 and 5 tonnes of food per day, depending on the species. These colossal creatures feed on small fish such as anchovies and sardines, but mainly on krill, tiny shrimp-like planktonic crustaceans which reproduce during the summer in polar waters. They may also swallow careless birds by mistake.

In its arctic larder, the humpback whale feeds on shrimp.

A sieve-like jaw

To fulfil such colossal dietary requirements, these large cetaceans have perfected an ingenious filtering system, which enables them to strain the sea water. When it opens its mouth, a baleen whale takes in several tonnes of plankton-filled water. Three hundred pairs of baleen plates (which can attain a length of 3 metres in bowhead whales) suspended from the upper jaw act as a sieve. When the whale closes its mouth, the sea water

Baleen whales have to surface for air.

The baleen plates of humpback whales are rarely longer than 50 centimetres. Made of horn, they are suspended from the upper jaw.

is pushed out and the small sea creatures remain trapped behind the baleen plates. The baleen whale simply slides them to the back of its throat with its tongue, then swallows them.

Sophisticated fishing techniques

Although all baleen whales filter sea water in the same way, some species have developed individual fishing methods. The grey whale, for example, swims along the seabed, leaning on one side,

Humpback whales may dive to a depth of 180 metres to feed.

drawing in water and sediment that contains the small crustaceans on which it feeds. The humpback whale prefers a more inventive technique. After locating a shoal of plankton, it positions itself beneath it and slowly swims upwards in a spiral, expelling air through its blowhole. Thousands of bubbles weave a net, imprisoning the krill. The whale merely has to open its mouth to swallow several hundred kilograms of shrimp. An even more effective refinement consists in five or six humpback whales collaborating to surround the

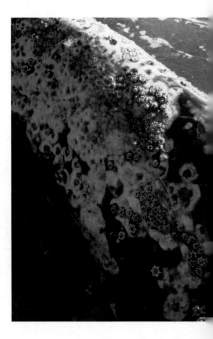

Seabirds show no fear of a baleen whale. They follow it, feeding on the krill and small fish that escape its enormous mouth.

▼ When baleen whales come to the surface, they violently exhale the air contained in their lungs through their blowhole, then immediately breathe in: this is the 'blow' or spout of baleen whales. The exhaled air produces a blast which can be heard hundreds of metres away. To avoid drowning, the blowhole is closed by a muscle which is only activated on contact with the air. The height, shape and direction of the blow varies with the species: bowhead whales emit two columns of spray while humpback whales produce a single jet.

Humpback whales in the frozen North fish using a 'net' of bubbles.

shoals of plankton and feed in turn. Their nets of bubbles can then attain some 20 metres in diameter.

20,000 kilometres to the breeding grounds

After a summer spent in the cold polar waters maintaining their layer of insulating fat by continual feasting, baleen whales are ready to embark on their long winter journey to warmer waters. Although the

A pair of whales setting off on their long migration.

The folds of skin below the throat of the baleen whale (long grooves) enable the mouth to open extremely wide and take in several cubic metres of water.

Long-distance migrations sometimes result in casualties.

tropical seas are not abundant in food, they are ideal for mating and giving birth to young. The most remarkable migration is made by the grey whale. Every year, it spends the summer in the Arctic, crosses the Bering Strait at the start of winter and travels along the west coast of America to arrive at its breeding ground in the warm Mexican waters of the Gulf of California. The journey will have taken three months and covered 20,000 kilometres.

A compass in their head

Every year, baleen whales follow approximately the same routes over the sea. To orient themselves in his watery expanse without landmarks, their brains contain small crystals made of magnetite (a magnetized iron oxide) naturally oriented towards the north like a compass. By assessing the changes of axis in these mini-magnets, the whales are able to keep heading in the

The arrival of the whales off the shores of Lower California signals the start of winter.

In the bright sunshine of the Californian sea, the whales enjoy a well-earned rest, before launching into their elaborate courtship rituals.

The whales will be able to devote their winter months in the warmer waters to mating displays, copulating and births.

Male humpbacks are extremely acrobatic when breaching (leaping out of the water). They make a thunderous noise when they fall back into the water.

All whales produce melodious sounds, but the humpback whale has the most beautiful voice. In this species, singing is largely the province of the males and serves, among other things, to attract the females. These songs are long, repeated melodic sequences with numerous variations. These sequences last ten minutes and can be heard within a radius of 20 or 30 kilometres. The same sequences are used by baleen whales from the same area, suggesting that several languages might exist within the whale kingdom.

right direction. In certain places, particularly where the underwater relief of the ocean is very pronounced, there are variations in the Earth's magnetic field and these are used by the cetaceans as underwater markers

Whales are born where they were conceived

Acrobatic displays impress the females and intimidate the other males.

Once in warm waters, the baleen whales breed. While mothers-to-be prepare for the birth of their calves – conceived a year earlier in the same place – other whales begin their sexual displays. The males are assiduous in their noisy, acrobatic courtship, which comprises songs and spectacular leaps. After lengthy displays with a great deal of rubbing and caressing, copulation takes place, during which the mating pair swim on the surface on their sides. The actual coitus is very brief, lasting only a matter of seconds. The whale calves already weigh over a tonne when they are born and are 4.5 metres long. As soon as they are born, the calves are nudged by their mothers

The calf never strays far from its mother and it imitates her every movement. In the warm waters, it conserves its energy for the long journey to polar waters.

towards the surface where they take their first breath. Suckling begins almost immediately afterwards, when the calf quickly finds its mother's nipple in her mammary slit. Every day, she produces 500 litres of milk which is rich in protein and has a high fat content. After six months of this gargantuan diet, the calves have doubled their weight and are ready to undertake the long journey to the icy polar waters.

Sometimes, the young calf is carried by its mother out of the water.

In the Gulf of Mexico, baleen whales enjoy a leisurely frolic in the sunset before mating: a tricky exercise which requires careful manoeuvring.

The grey whale breathes through twin blowholes on top of its head, so its unmistakable blow is divided into two columns of spray.

Whales and Dolphins in Our World

This fresco by Raphael was painted in 1512 in the Villa Farnesina at Rome. It depicts the triumph of the Greek goddess, Galatea, whose chariot is pulled by two dolphins.

Legends about whales and dolphins

Cetaceans have always figured prominently in the world's myths and legends. While dolphins are regarded as powerful symbols of friendship and loyalty to humans, whales, associated with the dangers of the sea, have long been regarded as terrifying monsters.

S EST ET ILLORVM ICON APVD EVNDEM, CAPITE, R
bus, fistulis, quos montium instar grandes esse scribit, & naues euertere, nisi sono tub
n aut missis in mare rotundis & uacuis uasis absterreantur : quod & in Balthico
mari circa balænam Brunfisch dictam fieri diximus.

In the Middle Ages, barrels were thrown into the sea to prevent whales, thought to be monstrous, aggressive creatures, from capsizing the ships.

D olphins and whales have fascinated human beings since time immemorial, occupying a central position in the beliefs of many coastal peoples. Dolphins were a common daily sight for the Ancient Greeks, and they acquired a place in their collective imagination. They appear on the oldest fresco, that of Knossos, which dates from 1600 BC. They were revered by the Greeks as messengers, communicating directly with Olympus. Apollo, in fact, assumed the form of a dolphin when he founded the famous Delphic Oracle. One of his companions, Delphinios, was a dolphin. The god of beauty regarded these friendly animals as the personification of virtue, love of humanity and enjoyment of life.

The Fountain of Neptune in Rome shows the god surrounded by dolphins.

Rescued by dolphins

Ancient legends from all the continents, including Brazil, Canada, Mauritania and Vietnam, describe the rescue of shipwreck victims by dolphins. According to Greek mythology, a dolphin saved

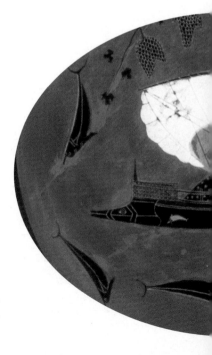

In Greek mythology, Apollo took the form of a dolphin when he founded the Delphic oracle. A small cetacean was carved on the pediment of the temple.

The story of Dionysus and the pirates is found in Greek mythology. Taken prisoner by bandits, the god of wine was tied to the mast of their ship. He proceeded to work a series of prodigies, untying the knots that lashed him to the mast and causing vines and ivy to grow. He changed the oars into snakes while he himself took the form of a lion. In panic, the pirates threw themselves into the sea and were changed into dolphins. Having repented of their actions, they now provide assistance to sailors.

Dolphins were worshipped in the Roman Empire and were used as a popular decorative motif in many of Rome's ancient mosaics.

Arion, a poet and musician thrown into the sea by barbarous pirates. Enchanted by the music from Arion's lyre, the dolphin carried him to the shore on his back.

A loyal friend

Friendship between cetaceans and humans is not only the stuff of legend but also well documented in real life. The Roman scholar, Pliny the Elder, wrote about a dolphin that had struck up a friend-

The dolphin was one of Poseidon's avatars.

ship with a young student and used to carry him across the Bay of Naples every day to school. When the young man was carried off by a fatal disease, the dolphin died of a broken heart.

Help for sailors

The people of Polynesia also admire dolphins: back in the mists of time, these animals guided them over the vast expanse of the Pacific Ocean by escorting their dugouts. Their aim was to find the

In the Middle Ages, dolphins were regarded as the lords of the sea.

Illustrations of Common Dolphins can be seen on the fresco at Knossos in Crete. As in many ancient paintings, the cetaceans' snout resembles a duck's beak.

Legend has it that, on a sea voyage, St Brendan, the 5th-century Irish monk and traveller, came across a whale which he initially mistook for a dark, barren island.

The Nootka from British Columbia (west coast of Canada), like the Pre-Columbian inhabitants of Peru, believed that the killer whale was a mythical animal, and revered it for its strength and courage. It appeared on all their totems and symbolized the close relationship between the cetaceans and native hunters. According to a Nootka legend, a white wolf with supernatural powers one day changed into a killer whale. Since then, killer whales have had white markings and roam about in packs.

Many Nootka Indian totem poles are decorated with carvings of whale hunters.

fertile island of their dreams. In sight of their promised land (modern New Zealand), the Maoris were swept into the sea by a hurricane. They climbed on to the back of the dolphins who took them to the paradisical shores of their new Eden.

Whales, man-eating monsters

Although dolphins have always inspired a feeling of friendship in humans, this was not always the case with their huge relatives, the whales. This can be seen from Western descriptions dating from the Middle Ages, in which terrifying whales with gigantic teeth symbolized mystery and horror. In the legendary bestiary of sea creatures, the whale was described as a terrible man-eater along with sea-snakes and giant squids. In 1555, the famous Swedish archbishop, Olaus Magnus, a scholar by trade, described one whale as having 250 horns over each eye that could be lowered at will like porcupine quills and eyes that were red and shone in the dark.

In the Himalayas, whales keep the Buddha company on almost all the sculptures in Nepalese temples.

The story of Jonas inspired many medieval illuminators.

From the Bible...

A fear of these monstrous whales probably inspired a persistent myth that occurs in cultures worldwide (including African, Lapp and Polynesian tales): the myth of a man being swallowed alive by a whale. The biblical hero Jonah was offered up to the raging seas to appease God, who was angry with him for disobeying His commands. Three days later, Jonah was pardoned and vomited out by the 'great fish'.

...to the Koran

In the Koran, the world is supported by a rather strange pyramid.

In the Islamic tradition, the whale has been in existence since the creation of the world, when the Earth hung just above the waves. Allah gave a giant the task of carrying the World on his shoulders and created the green rock for him to stand on. Allah himself rested on the back and horns of a miraculous bull. Beneath the bull was a giant whale whose convulsive movements were at the origin of earthquakes.

Legend has it that the whale was punished for swallowing Jonas: its baleens appeared, preventing it from swallowing anything other than small fish.

Before hunting the mighty whales, the early Eskimos first hunted small cetaceans like the narwhal.

Primitive whaling activities

Many centuries ago, courageous men hunted whales with basic weapons. The Thule people in the Arctic and the Basques in Europe pioneered a perilous type of hunting which appeared to be a one-sided fight that the animal had every chance of winning.

A slow swimmer living near the coast and readily approachable, the bowhead whale soon became a favourite target of the inhabitants of the Frozen North.

The narwhal was hunted for its meat and blubber, but also for its long single tooth or tusk, which was beautifully carved by the Eskimos.

The arctic peoples still hunt beluga whales today.

In the 11th century, the ancient inhabitants of the Arctic and the Basques of the Atlantic coast were among the first who dared to hunt these large cetaceans. Each of these communities developed traditional whaling methods that were well suited to their culture. During the polar summer, whales provided the Thule people, ancestors of the modern Inuit, with a year's supply of meat. The Basques saw whales as a inexhaustible source of raw materials.

Kayaks, vital to the techniques of the frozen North

When hunting small cetaceans, the Thule people used kayaks, lightweight sealskin canoes that were ideally suited for chasing beluga whales and narwhals. These kayaks, which were narrow, highly manoeuvrable, fast and silent, enabled the hunters – about 12 men – to form a line of attack in the open sea to beat their victims towards shallower waters. The frightened,

Inuit bows were made from baleen plates. The skin was used to make shoes.

Modern Inuit, like many indigenous peoples, still hunt large cetaceans. But their rare catches do not endanger the species.

Like their ancestors, modern Inuit drag their umiaks over many kilometres of ice before setting out to hunt bowhead whales.

It has been speculated that, well before the Inuit, prehistoric man hunted whales. The discovery in the grottoes of Le Mas-d'Azil in France of the 14,000-year-old carved tooth from a sperm whale lends weight to this theory. In fact, however, this tooth, with its carvings of ibex, was almost certainly taken from a whale stranded on the shore. The tools available at that time would not have allowed prehistoric man to hunt such powerful marine animals with any success.

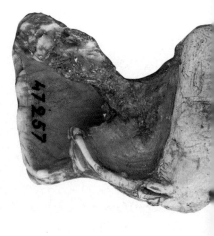

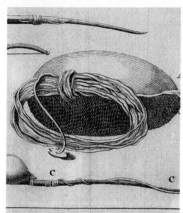

avec sa pointe, sa prise, & sa bouée. B.
inte, & l'Instrument pour le lancer contr
yeux contre la neige. E. Ornement de

nen punt, greep, & boei. B. De Pyl en
ug om hem op de Zee-Kalven te sch

Several floats of this type were needed to exhaust a whale.

exhausted narwhals and beluga whales were stranded in large numbers and killing them with harpoons became a straightforward task.

Hunting bowhead whales

Hunting large whales was quite another matter and required more sophisticated equipment and careful organization. When hunting bowhead whales, the Thule people added an umiak to their fleet of kayaks. This was an open boat that could accommodate up to eight men: six oarsmen, a helmsman and a harpooner. Approaching their prey in complete silence, the hunters usually attacked when it was sleeping. The harpooner darted it with a toggle-head harpoon connected by long ropes to a sealskin float so they could track it when it tried to escape. The marked whale was then chased by the hunters in kayaks who continued to wound it until it was completely exhausted. This hunt could last hours before the worn-out animal finally died. It was then simply a case of towing their heavy prize back to the shore where it could be flensed (stripped of flesh).

Whaling, a vital factor in the survival of the Thule people

Each whale killed was a godsend for the Thule people: a single whale provided 15 tonnes of meat for the village and 9 tonnes of fat that was melted down to produce oil, essential for heating and lighting. Whale bones were used for building the framework of houses, while the baleen was mainly used for making fishing nets.

The Canadian Inuit consider whale blubber, or muktuk, a rare delicacy.

Flensing the whale is an extremely delicate operation. Thick strips of blubber are cut widthwise, then sliced into smaller pieces.

The Inuit hunt bowhead whales in spring and autumn when they are leaving for or returning from their long annual migration.

The arrival of Basque hunters

In Europe, Basque sailors also hunted the bowhead whales which came in winter to breed in the sheltered waters of the Bay of Biscay. They gradually became expert at killing these huge cetaceans. Between the 12th and the 15th centuries, lookouts stood on high ground along the coast for six months every year to keep a close watch on the ocean. When a herd of whales was spotted

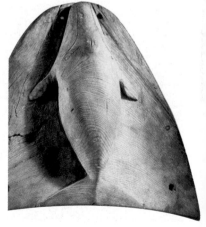

The Inuit show their respect for whales by depicting them in their works of art.

swimming offshore, they gave the alarm immediately by lighting large fires and banging drums.

The chase was on

Two or three rowboats were launched, crewed by a helmsman, a harpooner and four or five oarsmen. Guided from land by visual and vocal signals from the lookouts, they headed straight for the whales, the crew pulling hard at the oars until

The Basque sailors crossed the Atlantic in small ships.

The bay stations were a hive of activity. Whether towing whales, flensing them or melting down the blubber, everyone worked hard and pulled their weight.

Some people believe that the Basques, traces of whom have been discovered as far as Newfoundland, may have discovered America decades before Christopher Columbus.

they reached the open sea and the whales. When they came level with their prey, the harpooner threw his weapon. Wooden floats attached to the harpoon line impeded the panicked animal's escape, hampering its sounding dive. Bristling with harpoons and lances, the whale was finished off by a sharpened whaling spade, plunged into its heart by the harpooner.

The birth of commercial whaling

Some Indonesian fishermen hunt whales in flimsy boats.

Floating in a sea of blood, the corpse was then towed to the shore to be flensed at leisure. Day and night, in the heat of the melting houses, people cut up the blubber into large chunks to melt it in copper vats and salvage the precious oil. This, along with all the other whale products, was sold by the trading companies along the coast at the region's fairs and markets. This flourishing trade soon spread across the whole of France and Spain and whaling became a highly profitable business. The Basques had laid the foundations of the commercial whaling industry.

Indonesian hunters often return empty-handed. They have used the same methods for generations, but large cetaceans are becoming increasingly scarce.

Whales were hunted so intensively by the Basques in the Gulf of Biscay that, in the 15th century, they stopped frequenting waters they regarded as dangerous. Hunters then had to track them to their feeding grounds further north. In ocean-going ships they ventured as far as Iceland then, in the 16th century, into the icy waters of Labrador, where they built numerous flensing stations. Between 1545 and 1585, 17,000 whales were killed and processed in the Labrador bay stations.

HARPER'S WEEKLY.

JOURNAL OF CIVILIZATION

Vol. XXI.—No. 1069.]   NEW YORK, SATURDAY, JUNE 23, 1877.   [WITH A SUPPLEMENT. PRICE TEN CENTS.

Entered according to Act of Congress, in the Year 1877, by Harper & Brothers, in the Office of the Librarian of Congress, at Washington.

A WHALING STATION ON THE CALIFORNIA COAST.—Drawn by Present.—[See Page 485.]

Whaling was in full swing at the end of the 19th century. There was a sharp increase in the number of processing stations, like this Californian whaling station.

The golden age of commercial whaling

Between the 17th and 19th centuries, the international whaling industry went from strength to strength. In Europe, then America, wealthy countries built entire fleets of whaling ships. This 'oil rush' was closely linked to the heyday of the sailing ship.

In this 19th-century Japanese bay station, the whales were pulled up on the shore where they were cut up and processed to meet a variety of different needs.

Towards the end of the 16th century, Basque whaling activities ground to a halt: countless men and ships were conscripted by the Spanish navy for its wars with France. The English, Dutch, Danish, Norwegians and Germans took over from the Basques, gradually building bigger and bigger whaling fleets. The Dutch were the first to strike it rich when they discovered Spitsbergen, whose steep-sided fjords

As early as the 16th century, stranded whales were being studied.

The whale was left where it had been pulled up on shore for a couple of days. This time-lapse made it easier to flense.

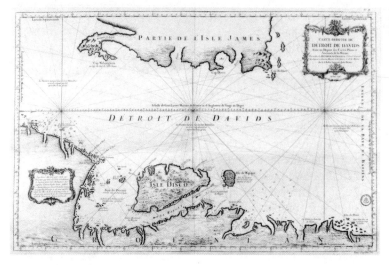

The icy waters of the Davis Strait, near Greenland, used to be plied by the Basques. In the 19th century, they became the hunting grounds for the European sailors.

provided a home for thousands of whales.

Harpoons connected to the fishing boats

Following in the Basque tradition, the Dutch pursued the whales in lightweight boats. As well as being connected to a float, the harpoon was now also firmly secured to the fishing boat by a line. After being harpooned, the whale now dragged the hunters' skiff behind it in its flight. As it became tired, it

Whaling was a complete eye-opener for the inexperienced.

resurfaced for longer and longer. The harpooner closed in on his victim and finished it off with a lance.

The first 'oil rush'

Either towed alongside a flagship or directly to the shore, the whale was flensed then processed on board or in the bay stations. These were like small industrial towns, buzzing with life at the height of summer and deserted in winter, with their collection of trading companies, bakeries, bars as well as the blubber-melting houses. In its heyday, the most famous bay station of its time, Smeerenburg ('Blubbertown'), welcomed over 15,000 inhabitants every summer as well as 300 whaling ships. This frenetic industry caused the bowhead whales to abandon Spitsbergen and emigrate to Labrador, which marked the decline of the Dutch whaling industry.

The birth of floating factories

The British colony of New England soon took over from the Dutch. From 1670, it was

When alarmed, breaching sperm whales may make spectacular leaps.

The corpse of a stranded whale in the Frozen North was a welcome source of food for hunters and packs of wolves alike.

The first ocean-going whalers could carry 2000 barrels of oil extracted from the blubber of around 25 whales. Assembling the barrels was a true art. These expeditions took coopers with them, expert craftsmen who constructed the barrels, often making use of the staves (ribs) and bottoms of barrels from the previous year. Before the advent of copper hooping, coopers used alder and willow branches that were stored in the ship's hold.

Whales were extremely abundant in the bay of Westmannshaven in the Faroe Islands.

the turn of the American ports to specialize in whaling. On board robust sailing ships, New England crews departed on extremely long voyages, following the migratory routes of their prey. Every whale they caught was flensed on board; the blubber was melted and the oil stored in barrels in the hold. Departing on a whale hunt, an American whaler might spend the spring sailing between the Azores, Guinea and Brazil, before returning to the North Atlantic

Harpoons had a toggle-head and were very unlikely to work free.

Whalers would set out for the feeding or breeding grounds where there was a high concentration of baleen and sperm whales.

19th-century paintings often depicted whalers hunting sperm whales, at the time regarded as the noblest of prey.

By its very nature, whaling entailed long hours of boredom while voyaging to waters frequented by cetaceans. As a means of keeping themselves occupied during the long days when there was no hunting, sailors used to carve baleen plates or sperm whale bones which they then sold in the ports along the way or took home to their loved ones. The most popular of these carved objects were 'scrimshaws', carved sperm whale teeth which often depicted hunting scenes or famous whalers.

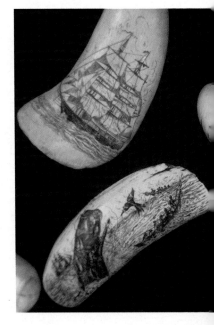

The bowhead whale was an easy target to hunt, and floated when dead.

for the summer. Stopping just long enough to unload its barrels and stock up on supplies, it would set off again for the Davis Strait, between America and Greenland, to cull transient whales which visited these waters. By 1750, bowhead whales had become very scarce in the Atlantic. To maintain their profitability, the Americans began to hunt sperm whales. In 1774, New England was the home port for nearly 400 whalers.

An English interlude

Beginning in 1775, the American War of Independence put a temporary stop to the American whaling industry. The English took over, discovering some new whale grounds in the Pacific, particularly off the coast of New Zealand and Australia. In 1815, the English lost this new monopoly as all their naval resources were required for the war with France.

The growth of the major whaling ports

The whaling industry under the fledgling American democracy experienced an

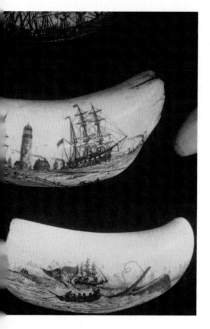

Accidents often happened. The sailors, who dreaded whales as much as the sea itself, lived with the constant fear of being shipwrecked. And few of them could swim.

Whale blubber was melted in large vats to salvage the oil.

unprecedented boom. From Maine to New Jersey, some ports serviced more than 700 ships. The largest ports were Nantucket and New Bedford. In 1857, New Bedford alone was the home port for 329 ships which roamed the world's seas with over 10,000 men on board.

$5000 per barrel of oil

The trade in whale products was now in full swing. Nothing was wasted and the superior whale oil, which burned without giving off bitter smoke, was regarded as one of the finest lighting fuels. It was also used as an industrial lubricant, because it remained fluid even at low temperatures. It was used for cooking, making candles, soap, paints, varnish and medicines. A single barrel of whale oil – one bowhead whale could provide a hundred barrels – was worth the equivalent of 5000 US dollars today.

Early 19th-century Japanese whalers.

The harpooner had to have a steady hand when hunting a sperm whale. The creature was much more resilient than other whales and defended itself vigorously.

From sperm whales to cosmetics

Spermaceti, the oil contained in the sperm whale's head, was even more in demand. This oil, when congealed at air temperature, produced a fine wax which was highly prized for use in the manufacture of odourless candles and cosmetics. Hand and face creams as well as many lipsticks made with spermaceti are still available today.

'Thar she blows! Thar she blows!'. Out at sea, a vigilant watch was essential.

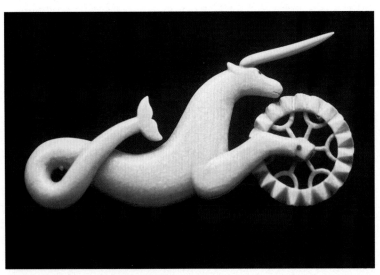

Sailors could fashion remarkable objects from sperm whale teeth, like this pastry-making tool, whose wheel was used to cut pastry.

After being towed by the whaler, the whale was securely lashed to the ship's hull and flensed from the deck.

Whalebone: from corsets to riding crops

Highly prized for their flexibility, the long baleen plates of bowhead whales had a variety of uses: processed in the whaling stations, they supplied many industries. They were used to make umbrella ribs, whalebone corsets, frames for suitcases, chests and women's hats, cane chair bottoms, riding crops, fishing rods and bed springs.

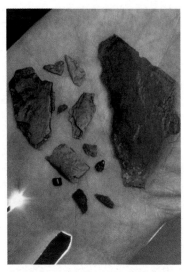

Ambergris taken from the sperm whale.

Sperm whale ambergris – worth its weight in gold

Ambergris was another whale product – thought to be formed from the ink of giant squids swallowed by sperm whales – which was regarded as an almost priceless raw material. Whale hunters were sometimes lucky enough to find this viscous substance in the sperm whale's intestine, which made the fortune of the entire crew. After a lengthy drying process lasting two to three years, ambergris was mainly used – as it is today – as a base for many luxury perfumes.

Moby Dick, the famous white sperm whale, was reputed to have acquired its colour from the many wounds inflicted by the giant squids and harpooners it had escaped.

▼ Moby Dick by Herman Melville, published in 1851, is a lively account of Captain Ahab's search for Moby Dick, the unassailable white sperm whale that had chewed off his leg several years earlier. In his writing, Melville drew on his own experience as a sailor (at the age of 22, in 1841, he set sail from New Bedford on the American whaler, Acushnet). He depicted detailed scenes from the hunters' everyday life on board ship, including the rowboat chases and the long hours spent waiting.

The men hunting sperm whales, like the Lilliputians capturing Gulliver, needed a great deal of courage to attack these monstrous creatures.

A treasure hunt

Whaling voyages could be very profitable. In 1851, the *Benjamin Tucker* docked in New Bedford with 300,000 litres of baleen whale oil, 20,000 litres of sperm whale oil and 15 tonnes of baleen. The sale of baleen taken from a single whale was often enough to cover the total cost of an expedition which could last 40 months. The rest was pure profit to be shared between the shipowners and the ship's crew. In a climate where everyone

In the 19th century, many American ports thrived in the age of the whale.

Except for the harpooner, the sailors on whalers were not experienced. They simply had to be strong rowers and able to follow strict orders.

The Scots also played their part in the whaling saga. This photo, taken at the turn of the century, shows hunters perched on top of a female sperm whale.

In 1864, whaling was revolutionized by a Norwegian invention: a gun that launched harpoons equipped with an explosive charge. Mounted on steam-powered whale catchers, this made it possible to hunt new prey, the speedy rorquals. When the harpoon buried itself in the whale's blubber, the sulphuric acid released set fire to a store of gunpowder and the ensuing blast caused instant death. Heavier than other whales, the rorqual had to be filled with compressed air to prevent it sinking to the bottom.

VÉRITABLE EXTRAIT DE V

III. PÊCHE À L

Courageous whale hunters were entitled to their own cemetery.

E : Le canon lance-harpon.

dreamed of making an easy fortune, the sale and processing of whale products had made New Bedford among the wealthiest towns of its time and the per capita income there was one of the highest in the world.

The decline of traditional commercial whaling

This golden age ended in the second half of the 19th century. The gold rush seriously challenged, then completely eclipsed, whaling in America. Popular wisdom of the time held that gold was waiting to be picked up from the sun-baked Californian soil and this seemed a much more attractive prospect than a whaling expedition to the world's coldest seas. Also, petroleum and its many derivatives had appeared on the market, making whale-oil lighting obsolete. The American Civil War (1861–1865) which commandeered many of the ships, did not help matters. Finally, the harsh winters of 1871 and 1876 delivered the death blow to the industry, as ice floes in the Arctic wrecked more than 50 vessels. This marked the end of traditional whale hunts.

Although they may enjoy performing, dolphins are still prisoners of the Dolphinariums, forced to take part in theatrical displays that are popular crowd-pullers.

Cetaceans in the 20th century

The 20th century has been a contradictory century for cetaceans. On the one hand, whales have almost become an endangered species due to relentless hunting but, on the other, they have been feted and given star billing, in the same way as dolphins.

In 1988, three grey whales became trapped by ice. After extensive media coverage, two were rescued by means of ice-breakers.

In the 20th century, whales became the target of a new, particularly intensive, type of hunting which used harpoon guns mounted on large fast vessels operating around a factory ship or a land base. Inaugurated by the Norwegians, quickly followed by the Russians and the Japanese, this modern technique butchered tens of thousands of whales in the space of several years. The aim was to obtain whale oil and spermaceti, which produced two

Discarded whale oil barrels claimed by rust in this disused Norwegian factory.

At an Icelandic whaling station, the carcases of two fin whales waiting to be cut up provide a feast for the seabirds.

Modern whalers used to bring back several dozen whales from each hunting expedition, seriously undermining the stability of the species.

The whales were flensed as soon as they were brought on board the factory ship.

superior lubricants, ideal for oiling missile or rocket engines. Finely ground whale bone was also used as fertilizer. Whale meat was used by traditional Japanese chefs to create new dishes and by Western factories to make cat and dog food.

Floating factory ships

These huge cetaceans did not stand a chance with the modern whalers, equipped with high-powered, explosive harpoon guns. Every whale killed was towed by a small launch to the factory ship while the whaler continued hunting without losing any time. On the factory ship – a huge vessel boasting a tonnage of 7500 and a crew of 400 – the whales were flensed and processed on continuous production lines.

Whales: an endangered species

These huge vats give an idea of the magnitude of the whaling industry.

Due to this high level of industrial exploitation, numbers of cetaceans dwindled drastically: it is estimated that there are now fewer than 2000 blue whales, as compared with 300,000 in 1930. Only 19 percent of the original common rorqual population has survived, while there are only a few hundred bowhead whales, the first to be hunted. In 1986, as a result of awareness-raising campaigns by conservation groups, public pressure forced a moratorium on commercial whaling which has prevented the situation from getting any worse, although poaching still continues in some areas.

Even today, some rorquals fall victim to lethal hunting activities which claim several hundred animals every year.

The International Whaling Commission (IWC) was founded in 1946 to tackle the problem of the fall in the number of whales. With 19 member countries, it establishes quotas, but is unable to police them effectively. Since 1986, only Norway and Japan have been authorized by the IWC to hunt several hundred animals for 'scientific research'. However, some argue that this has been misused as a pretext for commercial whaling, as these two countries had the right to produce meat and oil from the whale carcasses.

Before being flensed, the whale is hauled up onto a slope, a time-honoured practice inherited from the early whaling stations.

Dolphins under threat

Whales are not the only cetaceans to suffer at human hands. Dolphins have also become victims on the threshold of the 21st century. The main cause of death amongst Delphinidae is the excessive modernization of fishing methods. Every year, tens of thousands of dolphins become entangled and drown in drift-nets. These vast nylon traps extend beneath the surface for a depth of up to 40 metres and can

In the Faroe Islands, pilot whales are massacred by the thousands.

Many man hours are needed to flense the throat grooves of this type of rorqual, known as the minke whale.

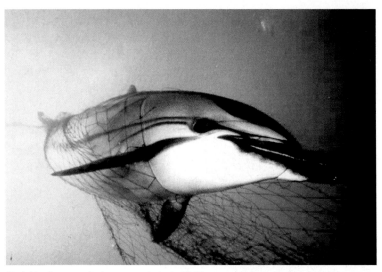

Dolphins become the innocent victims of fishing nets, as the sonar system of these small cetaceans cannot detect the delicate Nylon mesh.

It is quite common for whales to be found stranded. However, the stranding of sperm whales does not seem linked to pollution: according to ancient accounts, this used to occur before the sea became polluted. It is also unlikely that the once popular theory of suicide has any foundation in truth. In fact, mass strandings may be caused by a type of herd instinct: when the disorientated 'leader' of the group becomes stranded, the rest of the herd loyally follow, blissfully unaware of the danger.

Japanese fishermen are among the worst butchers of dolphins.

be as long as 20 kilometres. The pelagic nets used for tuna fishing represent another lethal danger. As dolphins tend to swim with shoals of tuna, fishermen follow them and then indiscriminately cast their nets.

Accusations of unfair competition

Other unscrupulous sea-fishermen regard dolphins as serious competitors and kill them deliberately. In Japan, blue-white dolphins are frequently beaten towards shallow waters where they are brutally massacred. The same thing happens in Sri Lanka, where more than 20,000 dolphins per year are harpooned along the coasts. In Chile, they are used as bait for crab fishing and around 50 dolphins are sacrificed to this cause each week.

Pollution, an insidious, implacable enemy

Marine pollution is another serious threat. Heavy metals, chlorine, pesticides, petroleum and other types of toxic waste become concentrated in the fish that are

the main food source for these small cetaceans. In 1990, as many as 740 dolphin carcasses were washed up on the Mediterranean coast. Their death is still 'unexplained' but there are strong suspicions that industrial pollution was to blame. In 1991, also in the Mediterranean, over 1000 dolphins died, this time victims of a virus whose devastating effect was undoubtedly aggravated by pollution.

Dead pilot whales turn the sea of the Faroe Islands red with their blood.

Victims of a mysterious malfunction of their sonar system, some dolphins venture too near to the coast and are stranded by the ebb tide.

No mercy for these unfortunate dolphins trapped with the fish in fishing nets.

In the Navy

Human beings have also exploited the intelligence of dolphins. In 1960, at the height of the Cold War, the first dolphins were conscripted by the US navy. For the first time, their remarkable sonar system was studied, and found to be more effective than any human device. But as they were unable to decipher the communication system, the Navy decided to train the

Like soldiers, the dolphins have been trained to mark out underwater mines.

American aircraft carriers at anchor were guarded by dolphin soldiers, recalling the Capitol's famous geese responsible for raising the alarm.

Beluga whales were also trained for war. During the Cold War, the Soviet army numbered scores of these unusual 'recruits' in its ranks.

Dolphin soldiers were retired from the American Navy in 1994.

dolphins to perform military missions.

War dolphins

During the Vietnam War and, more recently, during the Gulf War, 'American' dolphins, equipped with underwater cameras, were given the job of patrolling and guarding the areas around the US fleet. Capable of locating mines, some of these unusual, forcibly conscripted, 'service-men' were even used to salvage nuclear charges from the seabed. In 1994, under heavy pressure from the public and particularly in view of the détente between the two major world powers, the American Navy retired its dolphin soldiers. In total, as many as 240 dolphins served under Uncle Sam.

Whale watching: a new tourist industry

The heavyweight media campaigns conducted by conservation groups and countless television documentaries have helped to heighten public awareness of the unfortunate lot of whales and dolphins. The early 1980s also saw the worldwide growth of a 'green' tourist industry centred around cetaceans. Swimming with a dolphin has become a must, while going to see large whales is still an unforgettable experience. In 1993, more than four million people had become avid whale watchers, using a wide range of methods, from the simple inflatable dinghy to the converted whaler. Much more than a new fad, whale watching is a serious economic alternative

Whale watching is also possible from the coast.

Whale watching enthusiasts happily pile into crowded boats to watch their favourite creatures frolicking in the open sea.

Careful precautions must be taken when whale watching. Some devotees forget that these powerful creatures weigh 20 or 30 tonnes. In 1987, a grey whale in California capsized a boat with a flick of its tail, causing the death of three people. Off the coast of Hawaii, a diver was gravely wounded by an inquisitive pilot whale. These incidents have prompted some countries to impose strict regulations that ensure whale watchers maintain a set distance from the animals.

to whaling. Its international turnover accounted for 350 million US dollars in 1993. The Azores is the most successful example of this alternative approach: until 1982, people still practised traditional whaling in line with 19th-century methods. When Portugal joined the EEC, the Lusitanian government banned these outmoded practices and, in only a few years, the Azores archipelago has become one of the

In British Columbia, killer whales are easy to approach.

Killer whales are also highly intelligent. But to make them tamer and more obedient, their trainers deprive them of food.

On the walls in the town of Horta, in the Azores, traditional ex-votos painted in memory of dead sailors have been replaced by frescoes, some of which are in praise of whales.

most popular sites for watching large whales.

Dolphinariums, a cross between a zoo and a circus

Dolphins were first shown in captivity in Florida in the 1930s. Since then, the number of Marinelands, Seaworlds and other dolphinariums has soared, providing entertainment for young and old alike. These carefully choreographed shows provide a glittering showcase for

Alone in their pool, captive dolphins may become extremely bored.

This bay in Florida served as an arena for the daily frolics of Flipper, one of the most famous dolphins on television.

Killer whales have also had a turn in the spotlight; firstly, playing the role of the baddie. Disney capitalized on their evil reputation: in The Island at the Top of the World (1974), the heroes are attacked by killer whales in the icy waters of the North Pole. Orca Killer Whale (1977) is about a whale who hunts the fisherman who killed his mate. Dolphinariums have improved the image of killer whales, showing them as docile, harmless creatures. Free Willy, a recent film, painted an attractive picture of a killer whale.

dolphins and whales. There is only one problem: the stars – the dolphins – undoubtedly suffer in captivity. Fifty percent of dolphins in captivity die after two years in the limelight. The rest survive for an average of five years, while their free relatives live in the ocean for over 30 years.

The audience is probably unaware of the suffering of captive killer whales.

On the big or small screen

The beauty, 'smiling face' and intelligence of dolphins, which once fascinated the Ancient Greeks, have substantially contributed to the popularity of these friendly animals. Perhaps the most famous dolphin of all time, Flipper was the hero of the American television series of the same name. From 1963 to 1969, five dolphins performed in the title role. The film by the French director, Luc Besson, *Le Grand Bleu* ('The Big Blue'), is set around dolphins. All are friends of humans, coming to their aid or even saving their life. The advertising industry has also understood this trend, using this emotive image to target young people who are passionate about purity, liberty and integrity.

WHALES AND DOLPHINS
around the world

North
America

Atlantic Ocean

South
America

Pacific Ocean

Arctic

* There are two species of Pilot Whale: one is found in tropical waters, the other temperate waters.

Asia

Europe

Africa

Indian Ocean

Australia

	Dolphins
	Killer Whales
	Sperm Whales
	Baleen Whales

Antarctic

WHALES AND DOLPHINS
Principal Species

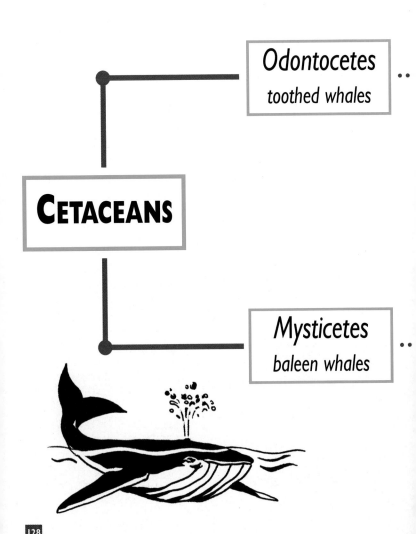

Odontocetes
toothed whales

..

CETACEANS

Mysticetes
baleen whales

..

Delphinidae account for over 30 species including the bottlenosed dolphin, which is the most famous.

The largest Odontocete is the sperm whale.

The killer whale is the largest member of the Delphinidae. Unlike them, however, it attacks other cetaceans.

The Greenland right whale or bowhead whale belongs to the Balaenidae family.

The blue whale is a rorqual belonging to the Balaenopteridae family, along with the minke whale and the humpback whale.

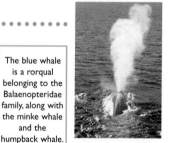

The grey whale, an Eschrichtidae, is regarded by some as a link between the Balaenidae and the Balaenopteridae.

Creative workshop

*Having studied all of these creatures,
it's time to get creative.*

*All you need are a few odds and ends and a
little ingenuity, and you can incorporate
some of the animals we've seen into
beautiful craft objects.*

*These simple projects will give you further
insight into the animal kingdom presented in
the pages of this book.*

*An original and simple way to enjoy
the wonderful images of the animal kingdom.*

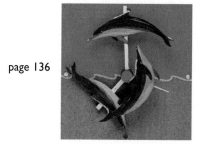

Dolphin Illumination

*A*n illumination is a miniature or a letter which the copyists of the Middle Ages used to draw in books. It will be a pleasure to decorate all sorts of objects – not just confined to the bathroom – with the precision work of this fanciful dolphin.

Drawing

Depending on the support you have chosen:
• If it is not possible to make a tracing, draw a square of the same size. Modify the line of one of its sides, as in the example, then draw the dolphin freehand using the example as a guide. The curve of the frame and the curve of the dolphin's body should balance and go well with one another.
• If it is possible to make a tracing, photocopy the drawings and reduce them until the central motif measures 5.5 cm on a side.
• Trace the border onto your chosen support, and then inside the motif trace the detailing and the outline of the dolphin.

Painting

• Using the large paintbrush, paint the dolphin in Payne grey mixed with white. Paint the background of the square in cerulean blue with a touch of celadon green.
• Pick out the lines of the detailing with a drawing pen filled with Payne grey or a blue felt-tip pen. Fill in using the same colour.
• Using the small paintbrush, pick out the outline of the dolphin in Payne grey.

The dolphin

• Using the small paintbrush, decorate the dolphin in Payne grey. You can follow the model provided, or you may prefer to create your own design. Use flat areas of Payne grey for the eye and eyelid. Paint fine lighter-coloured lines on top.

The waves

• Draw the waves in pencil on the blue background of the square, then paint the crests of the waves with

white gouache using the small paintbrush. Make a sort of fringe ending in flecks inside each curve, and add some stippling outside the curves.

Materials

- Two paint-brushes, no. 3/O and no. 6/3 • A sheet of tracing paper
- Gouache: Payne grey, cerulean blue, celadon green, white
- A set-square • A pencil
- A dark-blue felt-tip pen or drawing pen

Whale coat-rack

*T*he real D.I.Y. enthusiast will enjoy using their woodworking skills on the flowing lines of this pair.

• Photocopy the patterns, blowing them up so that the whale measures 38 cm long (1).
• Place the photocopy face-down at the bottom of the cardboard box. Spray its reverse side lightly with glue. Place the sheet on the thinner of the two pieces of plywood.

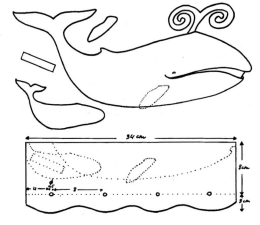

Cutting out the wood

• Clamp this sheet of plywood to a kitchen table, taking care to make sure that the part to be cut out is sticking out clear of the table-top (2). Saw around the outline (this is easier with an electric saw). Then cut out the whale calf, the fin and a chock 1.5 x 5 cm in the same way.
• Draw the waves on the other piece of plywood and cut them out with the saw.
• With a pencil, mark the spot for each of the four holes for the

handles and drill the holes using the 4.5 mm bit after first having placed a piece of scrap wood underneath to protect your work-surface.

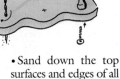

• Sand down the top surfaces and edges of all the pieces with the sandpaper.

Painting

• Paint the base and the handles green, paint the whales blue, keeping the belly lighter-coloured and paint the whale's eye, its spout and the baleen in its mouth white. Trace the dividing line of the tail with a brush-stroke of white paint.

Assembly

• Screw the handles onto their base (3). As shown in the diagram, glue the chock which will be the base for the whale calf to the lower left-hand side of the whale's back. Wipe off any excess glue with a cloth.

• Press the whale shape onto the base and make sure it sticks well by using

the little clamps at the tips. Then glue on the whale calf and the fin.

• Place the whole on a sheet of paper and place a large, heavy book on top to weight it down until completely dry. Nail two picture-hooks to the back to hang the coat-rack up (4).

Materials

• Two plywood off-cuts, one 3 mm thick measuring 40 x 20 cm and the other 10 mm thick measuring 34 x 11 cm
• A jig-saw with a fine blade • Sandpaper • Acrylic paint: blue, green and white (if left-over house paint is used, there is no need to varnish) • Wood varnish (optional)
• Two paintbrushes, one medium and one fine • Four medium cupboard handles with their screws • A gimlet with the same diameter as these screws • White wood glue • Two clamps • A glue spray • A cardboard box
• Two picture-frame hooks

Dolphin clock

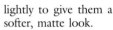

This deep-sea clock marks your day with the rhythm of a dolphin ballet.

Preparing the base

• Use the ruler and the lead pencil to draw the diagonals on the piece of plywood. Then draw the line of the horizon (a wave-like shape) and the vertical line.

• Mark the centre at the point where the diagonals intersect, and drill a hole there using the 10 mm bit.

• Drill a 4 mm hole on each side, 8 mm

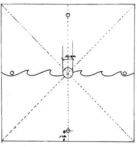

the edges.

• Paint the upper part – the sky – in blue and the lower part – the

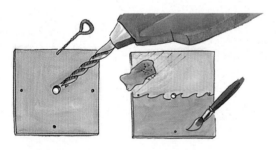

in from the edge, to mark the quarter hours: 3 o'clock, 6 o'clock, 9 o'clock and 12 o'clock.

• Sand down the surfaces, the holes and

sea – in green, not forgetting the edges. You might also paint the back in either one of these colours.

• When the paint is dry, sand down the surfaces

lightly to give them a softer, matte look. Paint little waves on the horizon (these can be varnished).

The dolphins

• Trace the dolphin patterns on to the Bristol board. Cut round each one with the scissors (if using non-expanded polystyrene, cut round them with a Stanley knife and then sand them down with sandpaper).

• Paint the dolphins in grey mixed with a drop of blue. Add white on the underside of the body and a few strokes of white to suggest a shiny appearance. Use a

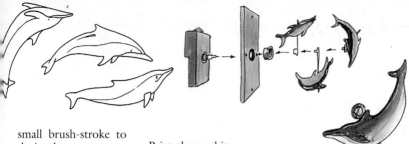

small brush-stroke to depict the eyes.

Assembly

• Remove the clock hands from the mechanism.

Paint them white.

• Unscrew the centre ring, place it over the hole on the decorated side of the board, align the clock mechanism,

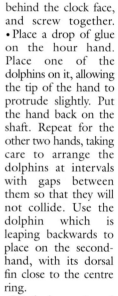

behind the clock face, and screw together.

• Place a drop of glue on the hour hand. Place one of the dolphins on it, allowing the tip of the hand to protrude slightly. Put the hand back on the shaft. Repeat for the other two hands, taking care to arrange the dolphins at intervals with gaps between them so that they will not collide. Use the dolphin which is leaping backwards to place on the second-hand, with its dorsal fin close to the centre ring.

• Put the battery in and set the clock.

Materials

• a small battery-operated clock mechanism with three hands (and a battery)
• a small piece of 3-mm thick plywood measuring 13 x 13 cm • Bristol board 0.5 mm thick (or non-expanded polystyrene) • a drill with a 10 mm bit and a 4 mm diameter bit
• fine sandpaper • a ruler • a lead pencil • scissors or Stanley knife • acrylic paint: blue, green, black and white • two paintbrushes, one medium and one fine • a small tube of very strong glue

Dolphin soft toy

This cuddly toy dolphin in soft shades of furry blue will be irresistibly huggable.

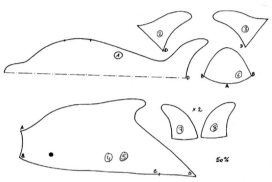

Preparing the parts

• Photocopy the 10 pieces of the pattern, increasing the size so the length of piece 1 (the underside of the body) is 40 cm from nose to tail.

• Cut out the pieces of the pattern. Pin them on to the reverse side of the cloth, and draw round them with the felt-tip pen, leaving a margin of 1 cm around each one.

• Cut out the pieces of cloth. Sew around the edges with zigzag stitch.

Sewing

• For each of the following stages, pin the edges before machine-stitching using a running stitch.

Making the fins

• Place upper and lower sides 7 right sides together and pin round the curved edge, leaving the base open, then machine-stitch. Repeat for pieces 8.

• Turn right-side-out and use a pencil to push the inside seam into shape.

• Stuff each fin lightly with kapok.

The tail

• Place the underside of the body on the table. Place parts 2 and 3 on top, one on either side of the tail, right sides together. Pin, then machine-stitch around the curved edge.

The fins

• Place the two ventral fins 14 cm from the tip of the snout, one on

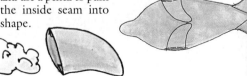

138

each side pointing towards the centre, and tack to close the hole and attach firmly to the underside of the body.

Materials

• a sewing machine with no. 90 or no. 100 machine needle • grey-blue fake fur cloth • matching thread • a felt-tip pen • dress-maker's scissors • pins • a needle • two black eye buttons • kapok or shredded foam rubber for the stuffing

The body

• Place flanks 4 and 5 right sides together, pin the top of A to D (with the dorsal fin) and machine-stitch.

The snout

• Pin the snout to seam B-A-B and machine-stitch.

The eyes

• Sew one black eye button on the either side of the piece.
• Turn this piece over and place it on the underside of the body right sides together; machine-stitch

the edges, beginning at the snout and con-tinuing as far as the points marked C (leave C to D open). Be careful of the extra thickness around the side fins.

Turn right-side-out, using a pencil to push the seams into shape.
• Stuff with kapok and hand-sew the edge between the two openings C to D on the upper side of the tail, using small stitches.

Acknowledgements:

The publishers would like to thank all those who have contributed to this book,
in particular:
Guy-Claude Agboton, Antoine Caron, Jean-Jacques Carreras, Jacqueline Damien,
Nicolas Lemaire, Hervé Levano, Marie-Bénédicte Majoral, Kha Luan Pham,
Vincent Pompougnac, Marie-Laure Sers-Besson, Valérie Zuber, Emmanuèle Zumstein

Illustration: Frantz Rey

Translation: Kate Clayton, Sue Rose - Ros Schwartz Translations

Impression: Eurolitho - Milan
Dépôt légal: September 1998
Printed in Italy